SIR TONY ROBINSON'S

WEIRD WORLD OF WONDERS

WORLD WAR I

Illustrated by
Del Thorpe

D0993943

MACMILLAN CHILDREN'S BOOKS

Thanks to . . .

If you turn to page 156 you'll find the name **Gaby Morgan** in tiny writing (in fact everyone who helped me with this book is in tiny writing except me, because I RULE THE WORLD!). Gaby is my editor, which means she tells me which bits of my books are rubbish and then makes me rewrite them. She's the biggest ever supporter of Weird World of Wonders, and is the best editor I could possibly have (although don't tell her I said that, please). Working with her is quite tough, but very interesting and lots of fun. Maybe I'll put her name in slightly bigger writing next time. Or maybe not.

I'm quite good at storytelling and making up jokes, but my researcher **Jessica Cobb** is a human search engine. If I ask her a question, her brain starts to whirr, steam comes out of her ears and she flips open her laptop, gets on the phone or rushes out of the room and sprints down to the library. Half an hour later she's back again, handing me the most brilliant, detailed answer ever. If I run out of cash I'll sell her to Google. They'll probably pay about a million pounds for her, and it'll be good value for money. Thank you, Jess.

First published 2013 by Macmillan Children's Books
an imprint of Pan Macmillan
20 New Wharf Road, London N1 9RR
Associated companies throughout the world
www.panmacmillan.com

ISBN 978-1-4472-2771-7

Text copyright © Sir Tony Robinson 2013
Illustrations copyright © Del Thorpe 2013

The right of Sir Tony Robinson and Del Thorpe to be identified as the author and illustrator of this work
has been asserted by them in accordance with the Copyright, Designs and Patents Act 1988.

5 7 9 8 6 4

A CIP catalogue record for this book is available from the British Library.

Typeset by Dan Newman/Perfect Bound Ltd
Printed and bound by CPI Group (UK) Ltd, Croydon CR0 4YY

Hello, we're the Curiosity Crew. You'll probably spot us hanging about in this book checking stuff out.

It's about blood, guts, mud, moustaches and millions of men making a military mess across half the world.

Read on to find out more . . .

INTRODUCTION

Ever since the olden days . . .

. . . the handsome prince raised his mighty sword . . .

Oooh!

. . . people have loved hearing stories about war.

. . . 'CHARGE' roared the evil emperor . . .

Aaaah!

Admittedly most of them had
never actually been to war . . .

. . . but the
bravest of the
knights stood his
ground . . .

Eeeeeh!

. . . and didn't have a clue
what it was really like.

. . . he sliced through
the emperor's armour,
sending his severed head
flying through the air!

But it all sounded exciting, heroic and full of glory!

Ahem!

But in 1914 World War One began, and that changed everything.

Suddenly hundreds of thousands of young men had to go to war, and they didn't like what they found when they got there. No excitement, no heroics and definitely no glory; instead . . .

And just to make things even more gruesome, a load of horrible machines and chemicals specially designed to kill people.

So, mixed up in all the mud were lots of bits of dead bodies and gallons of blood.

Human beings are stark staring bonkers!

It was horrific. Some people called it the 'Great War'; others said it was . . .

The
War
To End
All Wars!

But how did it start? How many people died? And who won?

If you'd like to know, turn the page . . .

CHAPTER ONE

HOW IT ALL STARTED

To the Black Hand Gang.
Read and Destroy.

Mission – assassinate the heir
to the Austro-Hungarian throne.

Date – 28th June 1914

Place – Sarajevo, Bosnia,
Eastern Europe.

Archduke Franz Ferdinand was a seriously important man. When his uncle died he'd become emperor of the massively powerful Austro-Hungarian Empire, which meant he'd rule over millions of people. So when he arrived in Sarajevo (pronounced 'Sa-ra-yey-vo') on a state visit, crowds lined the streets to catch a glimpse of him in his flashy uniform and his big hat with green feathers on it.

Archduke Ferdinand

Archduchess Ferdinand

Archmate of Ferdinand

Little did they know that among the crowd were six armed killers on a deadly mission. They were members of the 'Black Hand' – a band of young Serbian men who loathed the Austro-Hungarian Empire and were determined that their little country of Serbia wasn't going to become part of it.

THE EMPIRE OF NASTY SQUABBLES

Take a look at this map and you'll see that huge chunks of
Europe were once part of the mighty 'Austro-Hungarian' Empire.
More than 50 million people lived in it, speaking fifteen different
languages. It was big and powerful, but it caused lots of
squabbles, some of which got very nasty indeed.

Don't invade
us, we're only
little!

Their mission was to kill Franz Ferdinand, and because
no one in Sarajevo was expecting trouble, there were
hardly any police or soldiers about. It looked as though
this job was going to be as easy as squashing a fly.

But it
wasn't!

The first gang-member was just about to throw his grenade at the Archduke's car when a policeman wandered over to him. So the would-be assassin pretended he was an innocent bystander and walked away.

Franz Ferdinand's car passed the second gang-member, but he couldn't get his grenade out of his pocket in time, and the royal party drove on.

The third one managed to throw his grenade, but it bounced off the roof of the Archduke's vehicle and blew up the car behind.

Two more of these incompetent killers lost their nerve and ran away.

The last member of the gang, nineteen-year-old Gavrilo Princip, was really upset that their mission had failed, so he went off to a nearby cafe for a nice cup of coffee. But just as he was biting into his cinnamon and apple pastry . . .

We don't actually know that Gavrilo had a cinnamon and apple pastry, but it makes the whole scene a bit more dramatic, doesn't it?

No!

. . . the Archduke's car pulled up right beside him. Gavrilo jumped out of his seat, fired his gun at the Archduke and his wife . . . and shot them dead!

Even this murder attempt nearly failed because Franz Ferdinand was wearing a bullet-proof vest. But he was shot in the neck, so it didn't protect him!

The Archduke's assassination, drawn by someone who wasn't there

Whoops!

Not me!

Even though Franz Ferdinand's murder was horrific, who would have thought it would lead to the death of millions of people?

WHAT HAPPENED NEXT...?

The leaders of the Austro-Hungarian Empire were furious that some pipsqueak Serbian had bumped off the heir to their throne, so they declared war on Serbia. But it didn't stop there.

Austria-Hungary was friends with the Germans, so Germany joined in.

Germany was friends with the Turks, so Turkey joined in.

14

Serbia was friends with the Russians, so Russia joined in.

Russia was friends with the French, so France joined in.

And France was friends with the British, so Britain joined in.

Pretty soon the assassination at Sarajevo had turned into one almighty punch-up involving all the major superpowers of the time!

On one side were the 'Central Powers', including Austria-Hungary, Germany and Turkey.

Austrian troops march through Vienna in 1914

We'll beat those Brits in a week.

You sure?

The 1st Battalion of the Mid-Kent
Volunteers march through Tunbridge Wells
in 1914

THE BEST OF FRIENDS...?

The war was a huge surprise. Nobody could believe that so many European countries were fighting each other, particularly as most of the kings and queens were part of the same big family. This was all down to Queen Victoria of Britain, her nine children and her forty grandchildren who, like posh people everywhere, wanted to marry people as posh as they were – which meant other kings, queens, princes and princesses.

Happy Christmas Mummy from **Victoria** and **Frederick III, Emperor of Germany**

Happy Christmas Mummy from **Alice** and **Louis IV, Grand Duke of Hesse**

Happy Christmas Mummy from **Albert Edward (King Edward VIII of Britain)** and **Princess Alexandra of Denmark**

Happy Christmas Mummy from **Alfred** and **Grand Duchess Maria Alexandrovna of Russia**

Happy Christmas Granny from **Emperor Wilhelm III of Germany**

Happy Christmas Granny from **King George V of Britain**

Happy Christmas Granny from **Alexandra, Empress of Russia**

Happy Christmas Granny from **Marie, Queen of Romania**

Happy Christmas Granny

Happy Christmas Granny from **Maud, Queen of Norway**

Happy Christmas Granny

Happy Christmas Granny

Happy Christmas Granny

Happy Christmas Granny

Happy Christmas Granny

Happy Christmas Granny

About half the crowned heads of Europe were cousins, second cousins and third cousins once removed. They held family parties, sent each other Christmas cards and appeared to be the best of friends.

Happy Christmas Mummy from **Helena** and **Prince Christian of Schleswig-Holstein**

Happy Christmas Mummy from **Arthur** and **Princess Louise Margaret of Prussia**

Happy Christmas Mummy from **Leopold** and **Princess Helena of Waldeck & Pyrmont**

Happy Christmas Mummy from **Beatrice** and **Prince Henry of Battenberg**

Happy Christmas Mummy from **Louise** and **John Campbell, Marquess of Lorne**

Happy Christmas Granny from **Margaret, Crown Princess of Sweden**

Happy Christmas Granny

Happy Christmas Granny from **Victoria, Queen of Spain**

Happy Christmas Granny

Happy Christmas Granny

Happy Christmas Granny

Happy Christmas Granny

Happy Christmas Granny

Happy Christmas Granny

Happy Christmas Granny

Happy Christmas Granny

Happy Christmas Granny

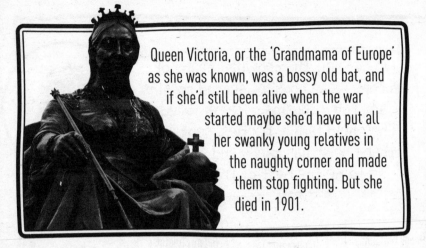

Queen Victoria, or the 'Grandmama of Europe' as she was known, was a bossy old bat, and if she'd still been alive when the war started maybe she'd have put all her swanky young relatives in the naughty corner and made them stop fighting. But she died in 1901.

WOO HOO - A WAR!

In August 1914, on the day war was declared, people across Europe poured into the streets to celebrate. Londoners gathered in front of Buckingham Palace to cheer, wave flags and sing the National Anthem. It might sound totally bonkers to you and me, but to many people at the time the war seemed a jolly good idea.

Just like today, most people lived ordinary lives in ordinary towns where nothing much happened that was remotely interesting. But now a big war was about to start just like they'd heard about in adventure stories. It was a chance for young men to be heroes, win glory and see the world. Best of all they'd get to teach those jumped-up Johnny Foreigners a lesson they'd never forget – hurrah!

King George V and the Royal Family watch a battalion leaving for France, August 1914

Of course, nobody considered for a moment that they might die . . .

. . . or that the Johnny Foreigners might turn out to be rather good at fighting!

They also didn't expect the war to last long – most people thought they'd be back home in time to put up the Christmas decorations. But they were seriously wrong!

... THE WORST OF ENEMIES!

Wilhelm II was the Emperor (or Kaiser) of Germany. He was one of Queen Victoria's many grandchildren, but he wasn't a nice grandchild: he hated the fact that Britain was powerful and had its own Empire. He was also vain, aggressive, tactless, boastful and rude, and called his granny the 'old hag'! Not surprisingly, Victoria couldn't stand him.

He encouraged Germany to build a big navy to challenge the British at sea. Britain and Germany had once been friends, but now they were the worst of enemies.

Kaiser Wilhelm II in the uniform of the 'Deathshead Hussars'

23

The chief officer in the British Army was Field Marshal Horatio Herbert Kitchener. He was a mighty hero with a big bushy moustache, who'd led his troops at the Battle of Omdurman in Africa where they'd won a famous victory!

Actually it was a famous victory which involved loads of British soldiers equipped with machine guns wiping out more than 9,000 Sudanese warriors armed with nothing but spears.

That's not very heroic, is it!

Kitchener had a niggling feeling that this war might be a bit different . . .

. . . because this time the enemy would be equipped with more than just spears!

. . . and he wasn't convinced the war would be over by Christmas. In fact he suspected it would last for years and that lots of people would get killed. He reckoned that Britain would only be able to win if it had a really big army.

He needed lots of young men to join up quickly, so masses of posters were printed with his big serious face staring out of them, and the words 'Your Country Needs You' in big letters – if that didn't scare people into volunteering, he didn't know what would.

But Britain's men didn't need scaring. They were simply itching to sign up. Kitchener had thought he'd be able to recruit 100,000 soldiers, but within two months a massive 750,000 had volunteered!

BOY SOLDIERS

It wasn't just men who joined up; plenty of boys did as well, some as young as twelve! To fight abroad, soldiers were supposed to be over nineteen, but lots of boys lied about their age, and in all the excitement recruiting officers often didn't bother to check their birth certificates before signing them up.

Some eager lads wore their Sunday suits or their dad's clothes to make them look older. Others gave fake names so that their parents wouldn't be able to find them and drag them back home.

COMPULSORY MOUSTACHES

Boy soldiers and women were pretty easy to spot – they were the ones without moustaches.

(Guess which one's the man)

It was a rule that all members of the British Army had to grow one, because moustaches looked so manly.

They look dogly too!

Women weren't allowed to be soldiers, but that didn't stop nineteen-year-old Dorothy Lawrence. When she was told she couldn't go to the front as a war reporter, she got hold of an army uniform, put a pair of socks down her trousers, cut her hair and cycled to the front line with forged identity papers which said she was Private Denis Smith! Unfortunately ten days later she was discovered and sent back home.

Anyone found shaving their upper lip was severely punished.

Eventually in 1916 this rule was dropped on the order of Lieutenant-General Sir Nevil Macready. This was partly because growing a moustache was a stupid thing to make people do, but also because Sir Nevil hated his own moustache so much.

It's like the small brushes with which kitchen maids and others clean saucepans.

He actually said that!

YOU'RE IN THE ARMY NOW

Soldiers were arranged into battalions of about 1,000 men.

That's wrong! Battalions started off with about 1,000 men, but after they'd been in a few battles, most had a lot less!

Brothers, cousins, friends, neighbours and workmates from the same town or village signed up together and formed what became known as 'Pals' battalions, because all the men in them knew each other. Ex-pupils from the same school formed battalions. So did professional footballers; even football supporters like the West Ham Pals!

Just imagine the whole Man U team and their fans forming a battalion and going off to Afghanistan!

KIT

Soldiers on both sides were issued with masses of kit, including:

Uniform – a grey-brown 'khaki' colour which blended into muddy landscapes. For a while British soldiers were the only ones to wear khaki. For the first few months of the war the French wore fancy blue coats and bright red trousers, until they realized this made them stick out like clowns at a funeral.

Webbing – a 'web' of straps that fastened round your chest and contained pockets and a rucksack to carry all your gear, including a water bottle, ammunition pouches, food, weapons and a blanket. Full up, your rucksack weighed as much as a ten-year-old boy! Imagine carrying one of those on your back all day!

Puttees (which means bandages) – these were strips of wool cloth that you wrapped round the bottom of your trousers to keep the mud and water from getting into the tops of your boots.

Steel Helmet – until 1915 soldiers wore a cloth or leather cap, but it quickly became obvious that you needed something more to protect your head from all those sharp bits of hot flying metal!

Scarf – hand-knitted by wives and mothers back home and sent out to the troops to help keep them warm, along with socks, mittens, balaclavas, woolly hats and sweaters!

Greatcoat – big, heavy and made of wool to keep you warm at night, with a collar or a cape to protect you from the rain. Got even heavier once you'd been standing out in the wet for a while, and took days to dry out.

Bayonet – fixed on to the end of a rifle so you could stab somebody if they got too close. Also used for digging holes, toasting bread, opening cans, poking fires and scraping mud off your uniform.

Tinned Food – invented in the nineteenth century as a way of keeping food fresh. Meals included corned beef, Irish stew, and pork and beans. The French army had tinned chicken in wine, and the Italians were given tinned spaghetti Bolognese!

Rifle – this was a soldier's main weapon. Its long barrel helped make it more accurate. You could shoot someone over 1,000 metres away!

Entrenching Tool – perhaps the most important piece of kit. A shovel that soldiers used to dig graves, holes for toilets and most importantly miles and miles of trenches . . .

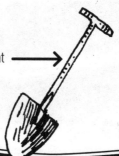

AN EMPIRE AT WAR

It wasn't just the Europeans who went to war. Many countries like Britain, Germany and France ruled over huge empires. The British Empire included India, Australia, New Zealand, Kenya, South Africa, Nigeria and the West Indies. Thousands of men from all these countries signed up.

Indian troops were some of the first to be sent to fight – 161,000 Indian soldiers called 'Sepoys' arrived in Europe in September 1914. The arguments between the British and the Germans didn't really have much to do with them, but lots of them fought heroically.

Australians leave Sydney on their way to Egypt

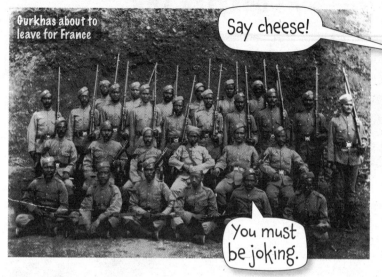

Gurkhas about to leave for France

Say cheese!

You must be joking.

During the Indian Corps' first battle, a Sepoy called Usman Khan was awarded a medal after he was wounded twice, continued to fire on the enemy and absolutely refused to leave his post. Then he was wounded again, and had both his legs almost blown off, but he still wouldn't leave the battlefield till he was dragged away protesting!

Although they risked their legs and their lives for the Empire, most colonial troops faced racism. Soldiers from the West Indies and Africa were called names, given poor equipment and had to do all the worst jobs like digging trenches, carrying supplies and cleaning the army bogs.

No wonder lots of them wished they'd stayed home and let the stupid Europeans fight it out among themselves.

CHAPTER TWO

DEADMAN'S DITCH!

At the beginning of the war Germany was almost completely surrounded by its enemies, Russia, France and Britain. But the Germans had a plan, and it was very simple.

They'd beat up their next-door neighbour France . . .

. . . turn round and attack Russia . . .

. . . and the British would be so frightened, they'd give in and beg for mercy.

So to put the first part of their plan into action, they invaded France. The British and French Armies tried to stop them, but within a month the German Army had practically reached Paris. The French military governor needed more troops to defend the front line, but there were no military vehicles available.

So he had a brainwave. He ordered a cab . . . well, more than one, actually.

Taxi drivers from all over Paris met at the city centre, and soldiers piled into them. Within two days, Parisian cabbies had dropped off 6,000 men at the battlefield, enough to stop the enemy in its tracks!

The German advance had been halted, but the Germans didn't retreat. Instead they dug long lines of trenches to protect themselves from a counter-attack. The British and French didn't know what to do, but while they were trying to work it out, they dug trenches too.

It was the start of **three years** of horrendous, bloody trench warfare.

HOW TO BUILD A TRENCH

1) Wait for nightfall – you don't want to work in daylight in full view of the enemy . . . that would be suicide!

2) Roll up your sleeves and start digging – there are no digging machines or dumper trucks: just you, your mates and some shovels. Stand in a line and shovel out the earth until you've dug a straight-sided trench ten feet deep and six feet wide . . . Phew!

3) Get in the trench – the sooner you're in, the safer you'll be. Now take turns to dig out the ends to make the trench longer.

4) Keep changing direction – you want your trench to be a zigzag shape, not one long line. That way, if the enemy manages to get in it, they won't be able to shoot all the way down it and kill everybody at once. And if a bomb hits, the explosion won't blow everyone up!

We also do decking for patios.

Germans in a very well-made trench

5) Fix planks of wood to the sides – this stops the trench collapsing and burying you alive. For extra protection put sandbags along the top to catch any stray bullets.

6) Put up rolls of barbed wire in front of it – this will slow the attackers down when they charge towards you.

And to slow them down even more, make sure you've got a few machine guns handy.

7) Dig another trench behind it – so if the front trench is captured by the enemy, there'll be another one handy for you to jump into.

The soldiers didn't just dig one trench, they dug hundreds. Soon the two sides had built a network of over 25,000 miles of them stretching from the English Channel all the way to Switzerland. There were so many that, in order to make sure the soldiers didn't get lost, signposts were put up, and the trenches were given names like 'Rats' Alley', 'Casualty Corner' and 'Deadman's Ditch'!

GROSS-OUT IN THE TRENCHES

The Germans were planning to stay put, so their trenches were built to last, with concrete bunkers, furniture, running water, electric lights, wallpaper, carpets and even doorbells!

But the British Generals wanted to attack the Germans right away, and they were worried that if their trenches were too cosy, their men might not want to leave them. So they made sure that the British trenches were not only basic, but . . .

GROSS! **GROSS!** *GROSS!*

They were gross because they were cold, dirty and wet. In winter the temperature dropped below freezing. Soldiers got frostbite and lost their fingers and toes.

Double gross because when it rained, the trenches flooded. Their boots got soaked and their feet started to rot. If they couldn't get them dry again, their legs would get so rotten the doctors would have to cut them off!

41

Treble gross because the trenches stank of decaying bodies, poo, rotting food and stagnant water.

Quadruple gross because of the rats. Swarms of them fed off the rubbish and the dead bodies. One soldier woke up in the middle of the night to see two rats on his bed fighting over a severed hand!

Some rats were the size of cats and would try to eat a wounded man if he was too weak to defend himself!

43

BRASS KNUCKLES

The ground between the two sets of trenches was known as 'no-man's-land'. It was covered with barbed wire, landmines, craters and dead bodies. To attack the enemy you had to cross it and risk being shot to pieces.

Sometimes hundreds of soldiers charged over it to try to force the enemy back. At other times, small groups conducted night raids to seize or destroy enemy equipment and collect information about how many people were in the trench opposite and how many guns they had. On night raids soldiers blackened their faces with burnt cork, and carried weapons that didn't make any noise, like clubs, knives, hatchets and brass knuckles.

Brass knuckles were lumps of metal that fitted over your fingers so you could give your enemy a killer punch.

THE DEVIL'S ROPE

In 1860 an American farmer called Joseph F. Glidden was looking for a cheap and easy way to fence off his land to stop cows from trampling through it. He came up with the idea of surrounding it with strings of twisted wire covered in sharp wire points. These fences were so vicious that the Native Americans called them the 'Devil's rope'.

In World War One, rows and rows of the horrible stuff were strung out in front of the trenches. It was difficult to blow a hole in them, and the only way to cut through them was with a pair of wire cutters.

Teams of men called 'wiring parties' were sent out at night to cut paths through the enemy's fences. They had to do it in total silence and in the pitch dark while handling sharp tools. You didn't live long if you were a member of a wiring party!

DON'T FALL ASLEEP!
DON'T GET LOST!

Discipline was strict. If you got drunk and were caught, you were tied to a wheel or a stake for several hours, sometimes in range of the enemy guns! The punishment for falling asleep on sentry duty, or for being a coward, or disobeying an order, was death by firing squad!

In September 1914, a nineteen-year-old called Thomas Highgate was found hiding in a barn. He said he'd got lost during a battle and was trying to find his way back to rejoin his unit. But he couldn't prove it because there were no witnesses; all his comrades had been killed or captured. So he was executed, and became the first British soldier to be shot for desertion.

FOOTBALL IN NO-MAN'S-LAND

It was pretty tiresome if someone fired a pot-shot at you every time you took a peek over the top of your trench. So sometimes soldiers on opposing sides would agree to have little truces. For instance they might decide not to fire at one another during breakfast, or not to throw grenades at each other's toilets.

Being shot at when you're like this is particularly annoying.

Sometimes after very heavy rain, the two sides would arrange a truce so they could pump the water out of their trenches. They did the same thing after a battle so they could collect their dead from no-man's-land.

On Christmas Day 1914, a big truce took place along large parts of the front line. German soldiers put up little Christmas trees along their trenches, and both sides sang carols and shouted 'Merry Christmas' to each other. Some soldiers got out of their trenches and exchanged cigarettes and presents! A few even got together and played a game of football in no-man's-land, with helmets for goalposts.

The Generals weren't too pleased when they heard about this. Fighting started again the next day, and the following year sentries on both sides were told to shoot anyone who tried to have another truce!

WORLD WAR ONE SLANG

Ordinary British soldiers had their own special language. Here are some key words . . .

Blighty – Britain. From the Hindu word 'Vilayati', meaning a foreign country. Originally used by British troops in India. Later a 'Blighty' meant a wound so bad that it would get you sent home.

Boche – A German soldier. From the French 'caboche', meaning 'blockhead'!

Brass Hat – A high-ranking officer. Officers often wore brass-coloured braid on their hats.

Bully Beef – Canned corned beef found in ration packs. From the French 'bouillie' meaning 'boiled'.

Hun – Another word for a German soldier. The original Huns were a tribe from Asia who attacked Europe in the fifth century. In a speech in 1900 Kaiser Wilhelm compared the German Army to the Huns and it quickly became their nickname.

Kraut – Yet another word for a German soldier. Short for 'sauerkraut' which means 'pickled cabbage' (a dish which for some reason the Germans found very tasty).

Napoo – Dead, as in *'If we don't get out of here fast we'll all be napoo.'* From the French phrase *'Il n'y en à plus'* meaning *'There isn't any more'*, which the British thought sounded like *'napoo'*.

Old Sweat – An experienced soldier.

Tommy – A British soldier. Came from the name 'Tommy Atkins', which was used as an example name on British Army forms, a bit like 'Joe Bloggs' today.

Trench Rabbit – A rat.

51

HIDEOUS MONSTERS

After a while the Allied soldiers began to realize that the enemy were just ordinary, decent blokes like themselves, but back home their families didn't. They thought the Germans were baby-murdering monsters.

The Germans cut the hands off tiny Belgian children!

No they didn't! That's a load of rubbish!

Exactly. But when countries are at war, their governments want the army to think the enemy are bloodthirsty maniacs. Their soldiers might not want to do any more killing if they know the other side are just ordinary people.

Yeah, that's why they spread horrible rumours about them. It's called 'propaganda', and it can be really effective.

Yeah! Dead effective!

The Germans bayonet babies!

In Britain, the government encouraged newspapers to write gruesome stories about the Germans, and printed posters showing them as scary devils.

It didn't matter if the stories weren't true, as long as they made people hate the enemy.

Anything German was suddenly HORRIBLY HORRENDOUSLY BAD.

In Britain, German people were beaten up. In Australia, towns and streets with German-sounding names were renamed.

And in America, hamburgers . . .

Named after the German city of Hamburg . . .

. . . were renamed 'liberty sandwiches'.

Frankfurters . . .

Which originated in the German city of Frankfurt . . .

. . . became 'liberty sausages'.

And German measles became 'liberty measles'!

This is stark staring mad!

Even the British King and Queen changed their name to make themselves sound less German! Their surname had been 'Saxe-Coburg' but they altered it to 'Windsor', and they're still called Windsor to this day!

BLOWN TO PIECES

For the best part of four years the Germans were stuck in their trenches, peering out at the British and their allies . . .

1914

. . . while the British were stuck in their trenches peering back at the Germans and their allies.

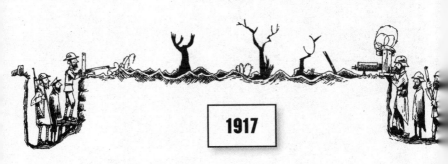

1917

Occasionally there was a big battle, but no one was really winning – at this rate the war would still be going on a hundred years later. How could the stalemate be broken? The Generals on both sides decided they needed bigger, better and nastier weapons.

WEAPONS OF MASS DESTRUCTION

Massive guns were developed which fired enormous shells.

I love enormous shells!

You wouldn't love these!

They were full of explosives, blasted massive holes in the ground and were designed to destroy the enemy defences. And to make them even nastier some were filled with bits of metal called 'shrapnel', which would fly out and tear through human flesh and bone.

The explosions from these guns were so loud they could make your ears bleed and, even if you weren't hit by a shell or bits of flying metal, the shockwaves from the blast itself could stop your heart and rupture your insides, leaving you dead without a mark on you!

The most famous German super-gun was called ... **BIG BERTHA**!

Big Bertha weighed as much as four double-decker buses!

Her shells were the size of dustbins, they weighed over 900 kg and she could fire them nine miles, high enough and far enough to go right over Mount Everest!

In one battle the British, Australian and Canadian guns fired over 4 million shells in two weeks!

That's 200 shells every single minute, non-stop, day and night!

YELLOW CANARIES

While the men were away at war messing about in their trenches, the women were working hard back home – driving buses, doing farm work, building ships, working in factories, assembling planes and making guns and bombs for the army.

One of their most dangerous jobs was filling shells with explosive powder. The women who did this were known as 'canaries', because the explosive turned their skin bright yellow. It was extremely poisonous and made you so sick you could die.

The explosives also had a tendency to go . . .

In 1917 an explosives factory on the edge of London blew up, killing 73 people, injuring 400 and flattening more than 900 nearby homes. The blast could be heard a hundred miles away!

An Indian Maxim team defending Egypt from the Turkish Army

DODGING BULLETS

An even more terrifying weapon was the machine gun, invented by Hiram Maxim in the 1880s.

At that time, even the most efficient guns could only fire half a dozen bullets, after which they had to be reloaded by hand. But Maxim's gun automatically fired hundreds of bullets one after the other. Even if you were a complete idiot you could become a bloodthirsty killer with no training whatsoever; all you had to do was keep your finger on the trigger!

The British Army bought lots of Maxim's guns, so the Austrians, Germans, Italians, Swiss and Russians bought lots too, and Maxim became a millionaire! By the time World War One broke out, all the major armies had machine guns. They were incredibly effective on the battlefield, killing tens of thousands of soldiers.

THE BATTLE THAT WENT HORRIBLY WRONG

In 1916 the British army planned a big attack on the German trenches near the River Somme in France. A week before it began, the Brits began firing their super-guns at the German trenches.

They had 1,500 of these massive weapons, and let loose 1.5 million shells. They were absolutely confident this bombardment would smash the enemy to pieces. They thought that when the guns stopped, they'd be able to wander over to the enemy positions, and the few quaking, terrified Germans who were still alive would throw down their weapons and run away.

But from the moment the first Brits popped their heads over the top of their trenches and started to walk across no-man's-land it became obvious that the plan had gone horribly wrong.

They hadn't destroyed the German trenches, which were very deep and well protected, and most of the enemy soldiers were alive and kicking. To make matters worse, the week-long bombardment had given the Germans plenty of warning that they were going to be attacked. When the British approached, the German machine-gunners opened fire and almost 20,000 British soldiers were killed! Another 38,000 were missing or wounded.

THE FIRE-BREATHING MONSTER

The very first flamethrower was invented over 2,000 years ago. Air was pumped into one end of a huge metal syringe, which spewed out tongues of flame from the other end.

But in 1901 the Germans came up with a modern version. It sprayed a continuous stream of oil out of the end of a tube, which, when lit by a spark, turned the oil into a terrifying stream of flame which could travel up to eighteen metres!

In World War One these fire-breathing monsters were used in the trenches. Anyone who had any sense legged it before they were burned alive.

GAS

Poison gas sounds really scary, doesn't it? But the gases used at the start of World War One were a bit pathetic. They made your enemy's eyes water and caused them to sneeze a lot, but that was about it. In other words they were rather annoying but certainly not deadly.

British gas victims in 1918

But then in 1915 the Germans started using chlorine gas. Chlorine is the stuff in your mum and dad's liquid bleach which they use to clean the toilet. It's great for killing tiny bugs that spread disease, but as any sensible kid knows, you don't want to play with it.

Chlorine gas is just as dangerous. It burns your throat and lungs, and causes you to suffocate to death very slowly. It was first released at a place called Ypres (pronounced 'Eep-rah'). Yellow-green clouds of the stuff drifted across the battlefield towards the French who, at first, thought it was just smoke. Then they started to cough and splutter and clutch their throats. Green froth spewed from their mouths and they keeled over in agony. Many died within minutes.

Chlorine gas was deadly, but if you released it when the wind was blowing in the wrong direction, you'd end up running away from your own gas.

I'm always running away from my own gas!

WEEING ON SOCKS

At first soldiers didn't have gas masks to protect them. Instead they were told that if a cloud of chlorine gas came towards them they should take off one of their socks, pee on it and put it over their mouths!

I do that too sometimes!

This is rubbish!

That may sound disgusting and a bit weird, but wee contains a chemical called ammonia, which was supposed to stop the chlorine damaging your lungs.

A bit better, I suppose.

Soon, though, scientists came up with less sick-making methods of protection. Early gas masks were simply cloth bags with eyeholes that you put over your head. The bag was soaked in a special chemical, which helped neutralize the poison gas.

Wicked, man!

But then they invented a 'box respirator', a gas mask connected to a box with a hose in the middle. The box filtered the air and made it safe to breathe.

Humans weren't the only ones issued with gas masks – horses, dogs and carrier pigeons got them as well!

HOW TO SEND A MESSAGE IN SCARY CIRCUMSTANCES

Just imagine – you're stuck in a hole in the ground being bombed left, right and centre, and you're running out of ammunition. There are no mobile phones, no computers, no internet, no walkie-talkies and nobody can hear you shout over the noise of the explosions. If you don't get help soon, you'll be going home in a body bag (well, bits of you will be going home, but some of you will probably be left in the hole for the rats).

So how exactly do you send a message saying that you need help?

1) Use a human – write a note on a piece of paper and get a messenger (called a 'runner') to carry it to its destination.

> Maybe not! Being a World War One runner is one of the most dangerous jobs around. Even if they run really fast, they'll be lucky not to get killed!

600-METRE MESSAGE MEDAL

In 1916 Sergeant-Major George Evans won a medal for bravery. He'd volunteered to take a message across the battlefield after five other runners had been killed attempting it. He ran across 600 metres of open ground while under fire, zigzagging and jumping from hole to hole for cover. Even though he was wounded, he made it there and back!

2) Use a dog – to avoid risking the lives of human runners, you can use a specially trained dog instead. They can run faster and are less likely to be fired on by the enemy. They're so useful that back in Britain stray dogs are being rounded up and sent to a special 'War Dog School' to be trained as messenger dogs!

No thanks! We can get blown up too, you know!

3) What about flags? – send a message in code using lots of different coloured flags.

The problem with flags is that you can't see them in the dark, and in daylight any arms that are waving them are likely to get shot off.

4) A torch? – soldiers have worked out a brilliant way of sending coded messages by using flashing lights!

But if the enemy knows your code they can read your message too!

5) A telephone? – you may not have a mobile phone. Never mind, though, there are telephone lines all across Europe.

But in an emergency there probably won't be a telephone nearby, and if you want one installed you'll have to wait for days.

6) A radio? – radio has just been invented.

But there aren't many of them, and they're bulky, difficult to carry and only have a short range.

7) How about a pigeon?

What???

What???

A pigeon???

Yes, use a specially trained homing pigeon. They're often your best chance of sending information in the heat of battle. Not only do they have a fantastic sense of direction, but they fly so fast and high that it's difficult to shoot them down. Over 100,000 carrier pigeons were used in the war and they had a ninety-five per cent success rate!

Pigeons win!

A MEDAL-WINNING PIGEON

In 1918 a pigeon called 'Cher Ami' ('Dear Friend') carried a message asking for help from a group of American soldiers stuck behind enemy lines to their friends in the trenches. The brave little bird was shot through the breast, blinded in one eye, and by the time she'd delivered the message, one of her legs was so badly injured that it was dangling from her body by a single tendon. She was awarded a medal for saving the lives of over a hundred soldiers!

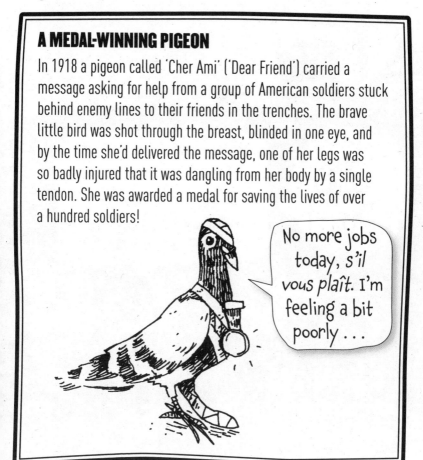

No more jobs today, *s'il vous plaît*. I'm feeling a bit poorly . . .

CHAPTER THREE
TWENTY
THOUSAND
GLASS EYES

In World War One millions of men were killed or injured. The statistics are mind-blowingly, knee-wobblingly horrible!

In 1915 nearly **2 million** Russian soldiers died or were badly hurt.

In June 1916 the Austro-Hungarian Army suffered **280,000** casualties in one week.

In August 1914 the French Army lost **211,000** men in sixteen days.

In 1916 alone the German Army lost **1.4 million** men.

On the first day of the Battle of the Somme in July 1916, **60,000** British soldiers died or were injured. This is the highest number of men killed on any single day in the history of the British Army.

By the end of the war **21 million** men had been seriously wounded.

Can't get a grip on those big numbers? Here are 1,000 crosses, which represent 1,000 dead people. If every page in this book looked like this one, and you bought 120 copies, you'd have just enough crosses for everyone killed in World War One.

Everywhere there were pools of blood, mounds of guts and piles of shattered bones. But behind the scenes thousands of doctors and nurses were doing their best to look after the wounded. And the good news is that because they got a lot of practice they became rather good at it.

Between 1914 and 1918 British doctors used 108 million bandages and 7,250 tons of cotton wool, fitted 1.5 million splints to 1.5 million broken limbs, and inserted over 20,000 artificial eyes into 20,000 eye sockets!

NO 999 IN NO-MAN'S-LAND

If you were hit by a bullet in no-man's-land your mates weren't allowed to stop and help you in case they got shot too. There were no emergency services to call and you couldn't ask your next-door neighbour to drive you to the nearest hospital. All you could do was try to crawl to safety and wait for a stretcher to come along.

The stretcher-bearers were under strict orders to look after the least badly injured first, because those were the soldiers who had the best chance of surviving. When your turn finally came, your problems still weren't over. It could take up to six hours to carry you through the mud to an ambulance!

LOTS OF BLOOD

Blood was a big problem on the battlefield. Adult humans usually have about ten pints pumping around inside them. They can lose one or two pints without too much of a problem, but if someone blows a big hole in their body, lots of blood will leak out.

It doesn't just 'leak'. If you get a really big wound in the wrong place it'll spurt out in big jets and you'll bleed to death in under a minute.

Shut up, Grace. This is a book for children, not vampires!

Can't I read it too?

Until 1917 the only way to replace lost blood was to connect a long tube to another person who had a similar blood group and take blood from their body.

Tell me more!

But this was a tricky process and relied on finding some nice person nearby who'd give you their blood at the crucial moment.

I love gorgeous people like that!

Eventually one doctor had the bright idea of collecting it in special bottles, storing the bottles in an icebox and transporting them to hospital tents near the front line, where they could be used when needed.

He'd invented the first blood bank!

Wow! That's my kind of bank!

Today all hospitals use blood banks to give them quick access to blood in an emergency!

That's enough about blood. Let's get on to the next bit.

WARNING: ACTUALLY THIS BIT IS PRETTY DISGUSTING TOO!

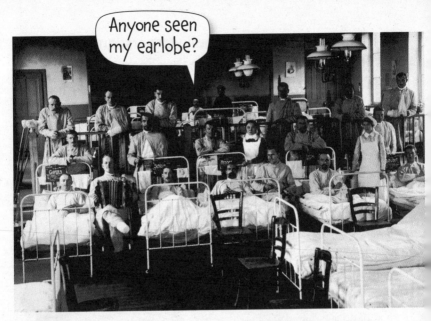

THE SHOP THAT SOLD TIN NOSES

Soldiers didn't just lose arms, legs, hands, feet and eyes; some lost their noses too.

Mirrors were often banned in hospitals in case soldiers with badly damaged faces saw their reflection and collapsed in shock. But some doctors were determined to try to put the battered faces of the injured men back together again.

Like all army doctors, surgeon Harold Gillies had a huge workload. For instance, after the first day of the Battle of the Somme he was presented with 2,000 new patients. Gradually he and his team developed ways of repairing faces, using pieces of skin from other parts of their patients' bodies to patch up their wounds and make their injuries less obvious.

But if a man's face was too badly damaged for this kind of treatment Gillies fitted a metal mask over his face which was painted to match his skin colour. Fake eyebrows, eyelashes and a moustache were then glued on to it using real hair. These masks were made in a workshop in a London hospital known as the 'Tin Noses Shop'.

GOOD DOG!

A German doctor called Gerhard Stalling treated soldiers who had been blinded. One day he left his dog with one of his patients. A short time later he returned and realized the dog was trying to look after the poor man. Did this mean that dogs might be able to help the blind? Stalling started training them and had amazing success. In 1916 he opened the first ever guide-dog school, and by the end of the war his schools were training 600 dogs a year!

A SPECIAL TEST FOR OUR FEMALE READERS

 Girls, if you saw a severed leg on the ground would you . . .

 A: Scream and pass out?

B: Throw up?

 C: Tut loudly at the mess, pick it up and put it out of the way where people wouldn't trip over it?

Sensible girls and women with strong stomachs were needed to help look after the sick and injured. They became nurses and worked incredibly long hours cleaning dirty wounds, bandaging bleeding heads and helping to saw off badly damaged arms and legs.

 If you chose 'C', you'd have made a great World War One nurse!

Some got awards for bravery. British aristocrat Lady 'Dot' Feilding received a medal for driving ambulances around the battlefield while being shot at, and Australian nurse Alice Ross-King was given one for staying at her post and caring for her patients while dodging falling bombs.

The despicable slaughter of innocent Edith Cavell by the hideously brutish, sneering, monocle-wearing, cigar-chomping, evil Boche. Note that one soldier is so ashamed of his villainy he can't bear to watch. This kind of exaggerated propaganda made a lot of Americans think that maybe they should be fighting the Germans too.

British nurse Edith Cavell is one of the great heroines of World War One. She worked for the Red Cross in Belgium, and when the Germans occupied it, she continued nursing there but at the same time secretly hid British soldiers who were trying to get back home. This was very dangerous, and when the Germans found out what she was doing, they arrested her, sentenced her to death and shot her.

But that wasn't the end of Edith's story. One of the reasons America finally joined the war was because so many Americans were outraged at the idea of a nurse being executed by a German firing squad. Her sacrifice was a big help to the Allies, even though she never knew it.

The memorial statue of Edith Cavell in London

SISSY PANTS?

Fighting in World War One was pant-wettingly, unimaginably terrifying, and many soldiers fell ill with a newly identified illness known as 'shell shock'. The horror of the dreadful things they'd experienced gave some of them weird facial tics. Others had terrifying nightmares and woke up sweating and screaming, or suddenly went blind, or couldn't eat, talk or walk.

At first doctors thought they were simply pretending in order to get away from the fighting. They were told to stop being sissy pants and to pull themselves together. Some were even shot for being cowards.

But a few wiser people said that anyone who'd been stuck in the middle of a battle surrounded by bodies, had been shot at and shelled, and had stabbed men to death with their bayonet, was highly likely to be driven a little crazy by the experience. In fact they thought

Treatment for shell shock included electric shocks

Pull yourself together, man!

Aarrgh! I don't think this is working.

it was surprising that every single soldier in the army wasn't shell-shocked.

Almost 80,000 British soldiers ended up suffering in this way and it was very difficult to cure them. Ten years after the war finished, 65,000 men were still receiving treatment for shell shock.

ATISHOO

But weapons weren't the only killers. Disease wiped out more people than all the shells, bombs and guns put together.

For instance, flu isn't very nice, but if you stagger up to bed, moan a lot, eat grapes and watch loads of DVDs you'll usually be right as rain again in a couple of weeks. But not if you lived at the end of World War One.

In 1918 a deadly disease called Spanish Flu hit the armies of Europe. Large numbers of soldiers from all over the world were living in unhealthy conditions in the trenches. This helped spread the flu virus really quickly. Soldiers caught a terrible fever and died within days. Armies on both sides lost thousands of men.

The flu virus looks something like this (though not as big, obviously)

Spanish Flu killed over 50 million people worldwide – more than the war itself!

CHAPTER FOUR
WAR
IN THE AIR
AND AT SEA

World War One didn't just happen on land. There were battles in the air as well. But flying in 1914 took a lot of guts, because planes had only just been invented!

The inventors of the first aeroplane were two American bicycle fanatics called Orville and Wilbur Wright. In 1903 they made their maiden flight. Their plane flew twenty feet above the ground and stayed in the air for a staggering twelve seconds!

That's a mighty odd bike, Orville.

Maybe that doesn't sound like a big deal, but it was the start of a completely new way of fighting wars!

They were made out of wood and cotton fabric, were held together with bits of wire and could just about carry one person – maybe two at a push. Frankly they were a bit rubbish! If you flew towards the ground too fast, the force could rip your plane's wings off.

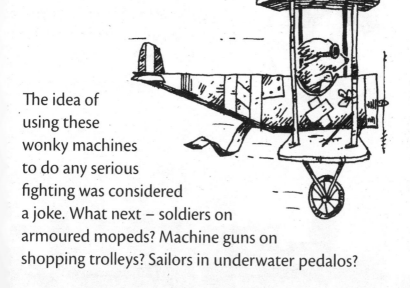

The idea of using these wonky machines to do any serious fighting was considered a joke. What next – soldiers on armoured mopeds? Machine guns on shopping trolleys? Sailors in underwater pedalos?

THE GOLDEN AGE OF AIRSHIPS

Most people thought planes were a gimmick destined for the rubbish bin of history, along with anti-fart underwear and washing machines for dogs.

Yup, somebody really invented both those things ... if you don't believe me look them up!

Who needed 'airplanes', when you already had large pointy hot-air balloons called 'airships'?

Airships were really, really, *really* large. Some of them were three times the length of a modern jumbo jet!

I've got a nasty feeling ...

They had engines to power them and propellers at the back for steering, with cabins underneath which could carry up to fifty passengers.

The Germans loved airships. They built some very good ones called 'Zeppelins', and when war broke out, they kitted them out for battle and sent them over to attack Britain.

On the night of 31 May 1915, a large, silent Zeppelin flew over London and began to drop bombs on the houses below, leaving seven people dead and thirty-five injured. Can you imagine how terrifying that was? Other places, including Edinburgh, Gravesend and Sunderland, were given the same treatment, and by the end of May 1916 at least 550 people had been killed.

As the war went on, new tactics were developed to defend the people on the ground. Powerful searchlights were constructed, and guns with special bullets blew the killer balloons out of the sky. By 1917 the Germans had given up using them for bombing raids, because they flew so slowly and made such an easy target. They were now a thing of the past. The future was ... the aeroplane.

SAY CHEESE!

Even though planes were flimsy and unreliable, might they be useful on the battlefield? Could they fly over enemy territory and take photos of what was happening below?

The answer was 'yes', but these missions weren't exactly a piece of cake. Not only did you have to fly in a rickety plane low and slow over enemy positions while dodging bullets, but you also had to hold your camera steady over the side of the plane to take the pictures.

And in those days cameras weren't teeny-weeny digital things that fitted into the palm of your hand. They were big wooden boxes, and you had to slot a heavy glass plate into the box, take your picture, remove the glass plate and put a new one in . . . all without falling out of the plane!

Pilots were only given a few hours' training before they were sent up in the air. No wonder so many planes crashed or got lost! In the early years of the war more than half of all pilots died in training.

And they weren't allowed to carry parachutes in case this encouraged them to jump out of their damaged planes instead of trying to land them safely. Aeroplanes were considered more valuable than pilots. No wonder they were known as 'flying coffins'!

COVERING A COUNTRY WITH PHOTOS

But all the effort was worth it. Photographs taken from these planes showed up all sorts of interesting things, like vehicle tracks which told you where the enemy had gone, or suspicious shapes that showed where guns were hidden. They could also help you make accurate maps, which were essential if you wanted to attack the enemy in a foreign land.

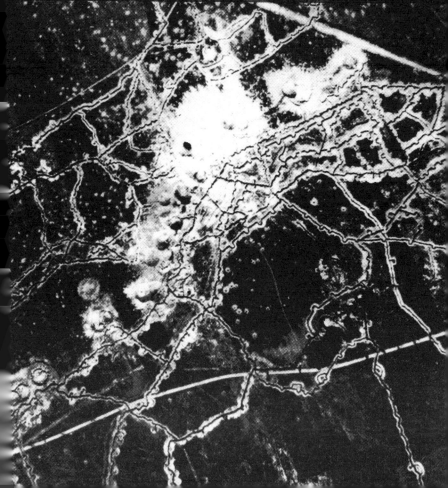

Planes became stronger and faster. Cameras also improved. Eventually photos taken 15,000 feet above the ground could be enlarged to show a single footprint in the mud below!

By the end of the war millions of aerial photographs had been taken. The Germans reckoned that if all their air photos had been laid side by side they would have covered Germany *six* times over!

NO MORE MR NICE PILOT

As more and more planes took to the skies, pilots from opposite sides began to meet in mid-air. At first they just smiled and waved. Then they remembered they were supposed to be fighting a war, so they started shouting insults and making rude hand signs. Soon they were throwing bricks and grenades, and firing pistols at each other.

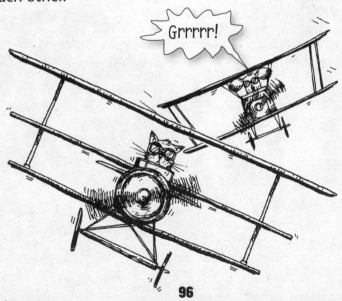

The first time a pilot brought down an enemy aircraft was in September 1914, when a Russian plane rammed an Austrian one. It wasn't a very smart thing to do: both aircraft crashed and the pilots died. But it was the start of air combat.

It wasn't long before planes were being fitted with machine guns. British pilot Louis Strange even fixed a 'safety strap' to his, so his co-pilot could stand up during the flight and fire his gun in any direction without falling out.

Two French airmen looking very silly

Serious aerial combat between
the British and Germans, 1915

British observation balloon and balloon shed, 1915

BALLOON BUSTING!

Each side had enormous observation balloons suspended above the battlefield, with a soldier in a basket underneath who sent messages down to the ground. These balloons were a tempting target for aircraft, and some pilots became expert 'balloon busters', flying at them and firing bullets until they exploded. Belgian pilot Willy Coppens held the record for the number of popped enemy observation balloons: thirty-five!

Balloon busting was a dangerous game. You could be shot down by enemy guns, or your plane's wing could get caught in the wire cables hanging between them. Sometimes decoy balloons were sent up with baskets full of high explosives in them which were remotely detonated if a plane came close.

THE RED BARON

No pilot was more famous than the German Baron Manfred von Richthofen (pronounced 'Rickt-hoff-en'). He was known as the 'Red Baron', and was so confident nobody could catch him that he painted his plane bright red. He shot down a colossal eighty British planes before he was finally hit by a single bullet in April 1918 while in mid-flight. He managed to land his plane safely near the Australian trenches, but died shortly afterwards.

The Allies were very impressed by Richthofen, even though he was their deadly foe. His flower-covered body was taken to an aircraft hangar, where soldiers filed past to pay their respects, and he was given a full military funeral.

A French soldier with captured German plane

Baron von Richthofen

COOL GUY!

PRETEND PARIS

Planes could also be used to drop bombs. In the early days of aerial warfare this simply meant flying over enemy territory and chucking one out of your aircraft in the general direction of your target. It wasn't very scientific but it could do a lot of harm.

Soon, though, aerial bombing became more efficient, and planes were developed which carried lots of bombs and could travel long distances.

They were called 'bombers'!

Eventually they were causing so much damage that the French began building an entire fake city of Paris to attract German planes away from the real Paris! They constructed pretend buildings and streets, and added realistic little details like making the windows of the pretend factories look dirty. Whether this would have fooled the Germans we'll never know, because the war ended before pretend Paris had been completed!

THIS IS PARIS.
No, honest, it is.

MEANWHILE AT SEA...

In 1914 the British Navy was the best in the world.
There was even a little song about it ...

> Everybody sing ... 'Rule Britannia, Britannia Rules the Waves ... dah dah dadadada dah dah ...'

Because Britain ruled the waves, it was able to seize the cargo from ships which tried to send valuable supplies to Germany.

Not only were metal, rubber and timber confiscated, but food was seized too. Soon the only coffee available in German shops was made from acorns, and the only bread was made from potatoes ...

> ... with the odd bit of sawdust or chalk thrown in.

The winter of 1916 was known as the 'turnip winter', because turnips were virtually the only real food the Germans had to eat!

> You'd have been happy, Tony. You love turnips!

> No I don't — shut up, Grace!

UNDERSEA PERIL

The hungry Germans got their own back by sinking Allied ships. Enter the most feared weapon of the war – the U-boat!

By the time of World War One submarines had come a long way since the not-so-deadly 'Turtle'. →
German U-boats were now made of steel, could carry more than fifty crew, could stay submerged for days and were armed with guns and torpedoes. They were also silent and could sneak up to a ship, fire a torpedo and disappear again without trace. Suddenly even the biggest, most modern ships were vulnerable to attack any time of day or night. How was the Royal Navy going to defend itself?

A German
U-boat, 1916

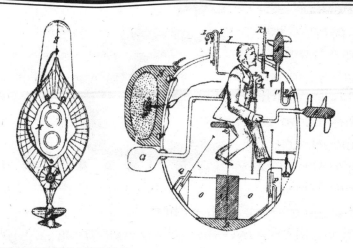

THE USELESS TURTLE

In 1776 an American inventor called David Bushnell built the 'Turtle', the world's first combat submarine. It wasn't very complicated, just a large wooden pedal-powered barrel with room for one person inside. A hole in the bottom allowed water to flow in so that it would sink, and two pumps were used to pump the water out again when you wanted to go back up to the surface. It could stay underwater for thirty minutes before the person inside the barrel ran out of air and brought the sub up . . . or failed to do so and drowned!

During the American Revolution Bushnell devised a plan to blow up a British ship in New York harbour. This involved getting the Turtle's pilot to drill a hole in the ship's bottom and then place a bomb inside. But it didn't work. The drill couldn't get through the hull. After that Bushnell tried to sink lots more British ships, but every time he failed. Eventually the British spotted the Turtle and sank it.

The ships' captains tried several things. If they spotted U-boats nearby they'd drop underwater grenades called 'depth charges' to try to destroy them, or attempt to run over them. They even strung underwater nets across the English Channel, so any U-boats that passed by would get tangled up!

But nothing seemed to work. Soon thousands of Allied ships had been sunk by killer subs. And it wasn't just warships that were under threat: all kinds of boats were attacked, including merchant vessels and even passenger liners like this one!

The luxury liner *Lusitania*

THE LUCKY CHAMPAGNE KING

In May 1915 the *Lusitania* set sail from New York bound for Liverpool. She was carrying 1,257 passengers and a crew of 702.

Despite warnings that U-boats were in the area, her passengers weren't worried. Many of them were American and their country wasn't involved in the war. And anyway the American multimillionaire Alfred Vanderbilt was on board, not to mention the so-called 'Champagne King' George Kessler, a wealthy wine salesman. The Germans wouldn't attack important people like that . . . would they?

Erm . . . well . . . yes.

The ship was travelling slowly through fog off the coast of Ireland when a U-boat commander fired a single torpedo at her. There was a thundering crack as it hit the side of the ship, which tilted sharply to the side and sank beneath the waves. 1,153 people were drowned, including Alfred Vanderbilt. (George Kessler was one of the lucky few who made it into a lifeboat.)

NOW YOU'VE DONE IT!

128 of the passengers who drowned were American. Back home their countrymen were furious! Anti-German protests broke out and Americans started muttering about teaching the Germans a lesson they'd never forget.

Even the Germans realized that sinking the *Lusitania* might have been a bad idea. They didn't need America ganging up on them as well as the Allies. So they promised to behave better in future and not to attack passenger ships.

But they didn't stick to their promise. By the beginning of 1917, German U-boats were again firing at any vessel that crossed their path. The outraged Americans declared war on Germany . . .

This was the best news the Allies could possibly have had. It was a bit like Superman announcing he was your new best friend. America had lots of everything – lots of food, lots of people, lots of steel and lots of money. And if the Allies were going to win the war, that's what they needed.

15 August 1917: American troops
marching through the streets of London,
watched by a welcoming crowd

CHAPTER FIVE

WAR ALL OVER THE WORLD

In countries all around the world there was heavy fighting . . .

... which is why it was called a world war!

There was fighting in Turkey . . .

The Turks controlled vast amounts of land known as the 'Ottoman Empire'. At its peak this empire had been one of the most powerful in the world, but by the time World War One broke out, it was old and weak.

The Allies thought the Ottoman Empire was completely useless and called it 'the sick man of Europe'.

So, late in 1914, the Turks decided to fight alongside the Germans. They thought Germany would win and if Turkey was on the winning side, the Ottoman Empire would become great again. But the Allies had other ideas. They were pretty confident they could make the Turks give in. So British, Australian and New Zealand troops launched a massive invasion from the sea at a place on the Turkish coast called Gallipoli.

This is going to be easy-peasy!

But it wasn't. In fact it was a massive failure.

The Allied soldiers were supposed to land on a gently sloping beach, but the current forced them north and they drifted on to a narrow strip of sand right under a towering cliff bristling with Turkish gunners.

The Allied troops were forced to dig trenches on the beach to protect themselves. These were even more of a nightmare than the French trenches, because in summer Turkey gets baking hot. Giant swarms of black flies covered the sweaty men, their food and the dead bodies which lay all around them . . . yuk!

The Turks up above blasted them with massive guns. Soon the entire shoreline was red with the blood of the helpless troops pinned down in their stinking trenches. Casualties rocketed. Over half a million soldiers were killed or injured. Reluctantly the Allies gave up and pulled out. What a disaster!

The Allied forces have landed in Gallipoli and are about to be slaughtered

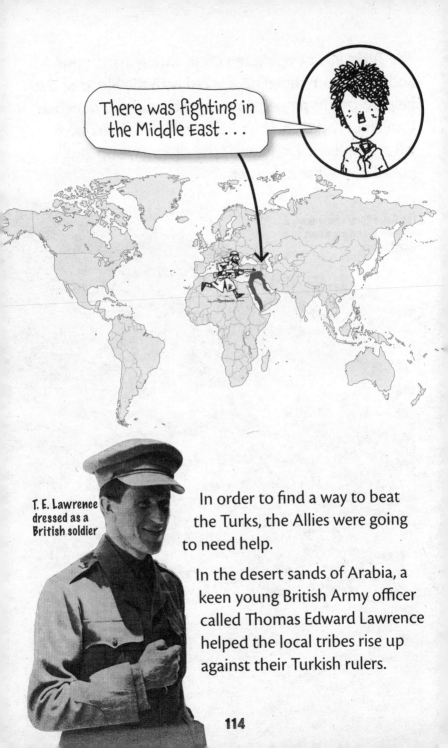

There was fighting in the Middle East . . .

T. E. Lawrence dressed as a British soldier

In order to find a way to beat the Turks, the Allies were going to need help.

In the desert sands of Arabia, a keen young British Army officer called Thomas Edward Lawrence helped the local tribes rise up against their Turkish rulers.

T. E. Lawrence not dressed as a British soldier

The Allies thought the Arabs weren't proper soldiers –
they didn't wear uniforms or fight in a disciplined way
like a European army, and they spent a lot of time arguing
among themselves. But an Arab warrior had skills which
were superbly useful in the desert. He could find his way
through miles of sand blindfolded, could dash across
sharp rocks in bare feet, and knew where to find food
and water among the bone-dry sand-dunes. Not only
that, but with a rifle in one hand he could jump on to a
running camel and escape in the blink of an eye.

A camel? What kind of soldier wants to ride a camel?

Watch it, mate! I'm the perfect desert fighting machine, me! I can keep going for eight days without water, I've got nostrils which snap shut to keep out the sand, I'm as fast as a packhorse, as strong as an ox, I can carry tons of equipment and can travel a hundred miles a day! Oh yes, and I've got gorgeous long eyelashes! How cool am I?

At first the Arabs were suspicious of Lawrence, but they soon grew to admire him. He gave them money and guns and showed them the best way to attack the Turks, travelling deep into the desert, blowing up railway lines, bridges and telephone poles, then disappearing into the sandy wastes like a mirage. And he never seemed to get tired; he once rode his camel for 300 miles without a break!

117

By 1918 the Turks had lost and the Allies had seized the desert lands which had previously belonged to the Ottoman Empire. But unfortunately that didn't bring an end to the problems of the desert people who lived there. The British and French had promised to give the land back to them, but instead they greedily divided it up among themselves, crammed lots of people from different tribes together into new made-up countries like Iraq, Palestine, Jordan, Syria and Lebanon, and expected everyone to get along. Unsurprisingly this didn't work very well and lots of fights broke out which continue right up to today!

FURTHER VIOLENCE

PROTESTS IN ISRAEL

BREAKING NEWS . . . BREAKING

SYRIA: LATEST UPDATE

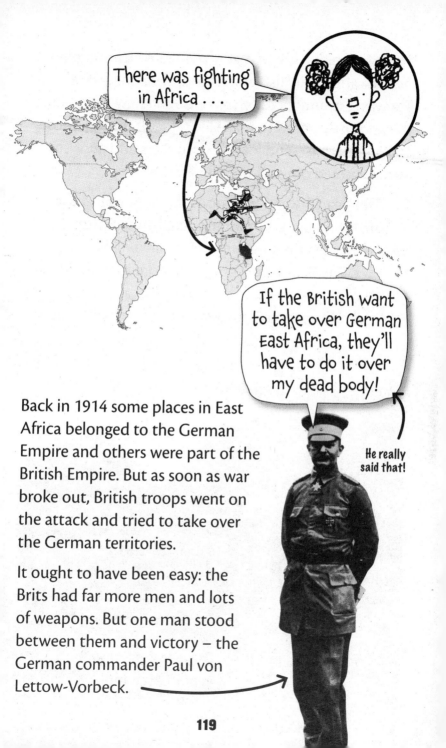

There was fighting in Africa . . .

If the British want to take over German East Africa, they'll have to do it over my dead body!

He really said that!

Back in 1914 some places in East Africa belonged to the German Empire and others were part of the British Empire. But as soon as war broke out, British troops went on the attack and tried to take over the German territories.

It ought to have been easy: the Brits had far more men and lots of weapons. But one man stood between them and victory – the German commander Paul von Lettow-Vorbeck.

He led a crack team of highly trained African soldiers and fought the British wherever and whenever he could. He was outnumbered ten to one and knew he couldn't win, but he wanted to make life difficult for the British, forcing them to send lots more soldiers and guns to Africa instead of using them in France.

For four years he and his troops ran rings round the British, leading guerrilla attacks, capturing British weapons, then disappearing before anyone had time to react. The British got more and more infuriated, but however hard they tried, they couldn't catch Lettow-Vorbeck. He became known as the 'uncatchable lizard'!

Make-up artist — my stripes are melting!

A pony disguised as a zebra for operations in East Africa

Imagine having to pull me out of your foot!

His troops were not only terrific fighters, but because they'd grown up in Africa they didn't catch all the horrible diseases that affected European soldiers. The Brits had a terrible time though. For every one of them killed in battle in Africa, another thirty died from diseases like malaria, sleeping sickness, and parasitic worms that burrowed into their bodies and feet!

The British never did catch Lettow-Vorbeck. When the war ended, the defeated Germans treated him like a hero and gave him a big parade. 120 of his men rode through the streets of Berlin, dressed in their tattered, tropical uniforms, and Lettow-Vorbeck led them, riding on a black charger.

The parts of France and Belgium where the Allies and the Germans were locked in deadly combat were known as the Western Front.

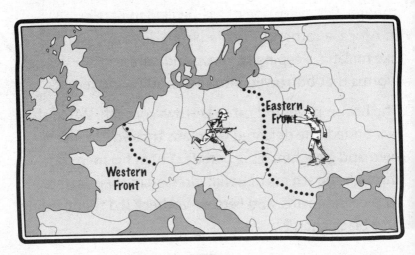

But there was an Eastern Front too. That was where the Germans were fighting the Russians.

The area over which they fought was massive. The Eastern Front was nearly 1,800 miles long, four times the size of the Western Front. The Russian army was also massive. The Russians had 6.5 million men, but only 4.5 million rifles.

HUNGRY LIKE THE WOLF

The rats in the trenches on the Western Front may have been pretty disgusting, but soldiers on the Eastern Front had to fight off hungry wolves! Matters got so bad that in the winter of 1916, German and Russian soldiers joined forces to defend themselves from crazed packs of wolves which were attacking their camps. Using poison, hand grenades and machine guns, they rounded up and killed hundreds of the fierce, furry creatures. Then they got back to killing each other.

Some Russian units were sent into battle completely unarmed and were told that if they wanted to defend themselves they'd have to take the guns from the hands of the dead bodies of the enemy. But even if they found a gun they probably wouldn't have been able to find much ammunition . . . which made winning battles just a little bit tricky. By 1916 the Russian Army had lost more than two million men!

Russian soldiers captured by the Germans in trench fighting on the Eastern Front

We may be prisoners . . .

. . . but it's much better than the snow and the wolves!

Meanwhile in Russian cities the transport systems were collapsing, prices were rising, criminals ruled the streets, and people were running out of food. Women in St Petersburg had to queue for food for forty hours a week (which is longer than most of you spend at school!).

What are we queueing for?

Bread.

A bus.

One Direction tickets.

THE LOONY MONK

The Russian ruler was Tsar Nicholas II.

Tsar, pronounced 'Zar', is Russian for Emperor.

Long hair

Craaaazy eyes

Big beard

Unfortunately for Russia, he and his wife had come under the influence of a weird, wandering holy man called Grigori Rasputin.

The Tsar and Tsarina took Rasputin's advice on how to run the country and fight the war. But the Russian people thought they were completely bonkers for listening to a mad monk, and in 1916 a group of Russian nobles invited Rasputin to dinner and murdered him.

Boy, did he take some killing!

They put poison in his pastries and in his wine, fired bullets into him, beat him with a club, and finally (just to make really sure he was dead) tied him up and dumped him in a freezing river.

Women soldiers fighting in the Russian Revolution of 1917

By 1917 the people of Russia were fed up to the back teeth with their stupid Tsar and his stupid war. In the city of St Petersburg, there was a big riot, and when the Tsar sent troops in to try and stop it, the army joined the rioters!

It was total chaos. The Tsar and his wife went into hiding and Russia pulled out of the war.

Tsar Nicholas II, with his family, on the roof of Tobolsk Prison following the Russian Revolution

CHAPTER SIX

THE ULTIMATE SECRET SUPER WEAPON

Meanwhile on the Western Front the opposing armies were *still* stuck in their trenches.

1918

But now, because the Russians had given in, Germany didn't have to fight on two fronts any more. Its troops swept west to smash through the Western Front and win the war once and for all.

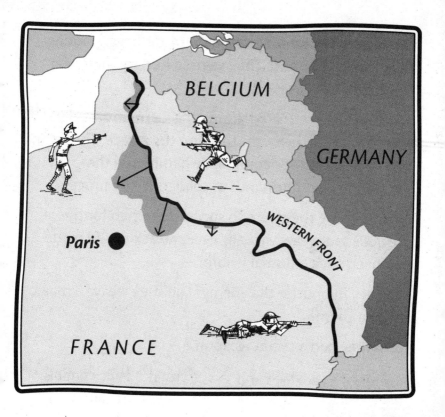

They launched a series of deadly attacks, broke through the Allied defences and continued their advance at top speed. Germany was now so confident it was going to win the war that on 24 March the Kaiser declared a national holiday!

But he'd made a big mistake. Very soon the Germans had used up all their food and ammunition, and the trucks carrying fresh supplies and weapons couldn't get through to the advancing soldiers.

Things quickly went pear-shaped.

Exhausted and starving German troops began looting Allied stores for food. They were so hungry they even ate their own horses.

The Allies had retreated during the German assault, but now it was their turn to go on the attack. They won victory after victory, completely hammered the German army and killed thousands of soldiers in the process.

So how come they were so successful, when for the previous four years virtually every attack they'd made had been such a dismal failure?

Did they hypnotize the enemy? Did they weave a magic spell on them?

No – they had a secret weapon.

German storm troops defend a series of shallow holes in the mud

What's that coming over the hill? Is it a horse? Great, I'm starving!

THE BATTLE OF AMIENS – THE BEGINNING

On 8 August 1918, at a place called Amiens in northern France, a massive force of Allied troops prepared to attack the German trenches.

Over the previous four years there had been hundreds of similar attacks, but thick barbed wire, deep trenches and lines of machine guns had made it almost impossible to break through.

This attack would be different though.

No guns were fired until the moment the battle began (which meant the enemy wasn't ready for an attack)!

Lots of bombs were dropped to soften up the enemy.

The army wasn't sent in first . . .

Instead, in the early-morning mist, the terrifying rumbling of the new super weapon echoed across the fields of Amiens.

Very poetic, Jojo!

Thanks!

The Allies' new secret super weapon was . . . **tanks**! Their massive size and enormous treads allowed them to smash through barbed wire, roll over trenches and demolish machine-gun positions with a metallic crunching noise.

THE LIGHT-BULB MOMENT

And how had British boffins come up with the idea of inventing such a terrifying new weapon?

The answer is . . . tractors!

Yes, folks, we were the inspiration!

From early in the war, tractors with caterpillar treads were used to haul big guns around the battlefield. They were perfect for the job because they were the only vehicles that didn't get stuck in muddy ground.

So . . . PING!

How about building a bulletproof tractor with a gun on the front?

This was a genuine light-bulb moment!

The British secretly began work on an armour-plated, tractory-gunny, German-squishing super machine, which at first they called the 'Landship'. But they soon changed its name . . .

It doesn't look like an armour-plated, tractory-gunny, German-squishing super machine at all. It looks like something to keep water in.

Hmmm! Wouldn't it be a good idea if the Germans thought we were trying to invent something to keep water in rather than an armour-plated, tractory-gunny, German-squishing super machine?

Yes, an excellent idea! Let's call it the 'Thing to Keep Water In'.

That's rubbish!

The first tank rolled off the production line on 8 September 1916 – Hooray!

Two days later its tracks fell off – Boo!

But the British repaired it – Hooray!

And it broke down again – Boo!

Making a reliable tank wasn't going to be easy.

Tanks were first used in battle in 1916. But most of them broke down repeatedly. If they were driven over swampy ground they sank, and even on good ground they were really slow.

And that was just the start of the problems . . .

A tank needed lots of people to make it work – a driver, someone to work the brakes, two people to change the gears and four to fire the guns.

The engine was situated right next to the crew-members, making everything noisy, hot and cramped.

In battle every hatch, flap and door was shut to protect it from attack. But this meant that the people inside could pass out, because the fumes from the engine were so lethal.

And it was pitch black inside your tank, so you had to learn how to drive it by touch alone.

And to cap it all, tanks were massively vulnerable to attack. They made easy targets because they were so big and slow, and if one was hit by a shell it could burst into flames.

And as they only had tiny escape hatches crews sometimes got trapped inside and burned to death.

MY GANG'S BIGGER THAN YOUR GANG

When the Germans finally realized what the Allies were up to, they tried to develop tanks too . . . but it was too late. By the end of the war the British and French had built over 5,000, while the Germans had only twenty!

THE BATTLE OF AMIENS - THE END

Eventually, by 1918, the boffins had made lots of improvements, they'd cracked most of the technical problems, and the Allies finally had enough reliable

tanks to launch an effective attack. At Amiens 580 of them led the way. They broke through the enemy lines and advanced so quickly that one party of German officers was captured while they were still eating their breakfast!

On that first day of battle the Allies advanced over seven miles, taking 17,000 German prisoners and killing or wounding 30,000 more! It became known as the 'Black Day of the German Army'. Imagine how excited the Allies were – suddenly an end to the agony of trench warfare seemed possible! With tanks and aircraft they might just win the war and finally be able to go home!

BREAKING THE HINDENBURG LINE

But not just yet.

There was still one big problem –
the 'Hindenburg Line' . . .

. . . named after the man
who ordered it to be built,
the head of the German
army, Paul von Hindenburg.

It was a network of deep concrete trenches up to
fifteen feet deep and twelve feet wide, surrounded
by a wall of barbed wire sixty feet thick, with
a 'battle zone' of over a mile in front of it
guarded by machine guns and artillery.

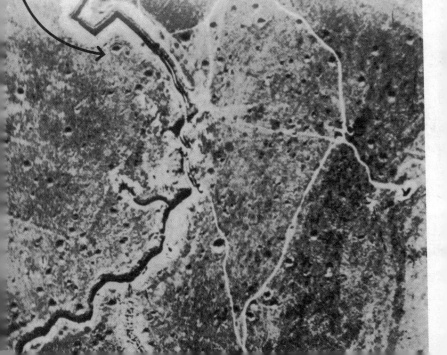

British, Australian, French and American forces launched an attack on it. They used their big guns first to try to smash it. Then tanks and aircraft supported the soldiers as they advanced against the concrete trenches. On 29 September they finally broke through! The Germans were beaten. Within days they surrendered. The Allies had won!

France, 1918: all that's left
here is destruction

Sgt. J. W. Milner.   Pte. G. E. Ellison.   Pte. H. Jubb.

THE UNLUCKIEST MAN

Perhaps the unluckiest man in the whole war was George Edwin Ellison. He'd been fighting since 1914 and had lived through some pretty hairy battles, but was shot dead by the enemy while on patrol just an hour and a half before the war ended.

WHAT HAPPENED NEXT?

The war had cost billions and billions of pounds. Millions had lost their lives. The world would never be the same again.

Most soldiers went home and tried to forget about all the horrible things they'd seen and done.

GRANDPA JACK

BABY ME

My Grandpa Jack came back to London from the trenches in 1918, threw his uniform on the sitting-room fire, watched it burn and never spoke about the war ever again.

Over the next few years people kicked out lots of the kings and emperors who'd dragged their country into this stupid war, and tried to make sure that in future they'd be ruled by ordinary folk instead.

THE UNLUCKIEST COW

So many bombs and mines were used in World War One that a few still pose a danger today. Some years ago a bolt of lightning set off an old World War One mine in Belgium and killed a cow!

Old and mighty empires like the Ottoman Empire and the Austro-Hungarian Empire collapsed, and the Russians got rid of Tsar Nicholas. He was executed along with his family in July 1918.

Kaiser Wilhelm of Germany was booted out too, but lots of Germans were still very angry. They thought they should have won, and sincerely believed they would have done so if they'd been allowed to keep on fighting.

Just twenty years later Germany was ready to fight again, and this time an even bigger and deadlier war broke out.

But that's another story . . .

TIMELINE

28 Jun 1914 The Austro-Hungarian nobleman Archduke Franz Ferdinand is assassinated in Sarajevo

Aug 1914 War is declared

Sep 1914 The armies dig into their trenches

1915 Allied soldiers are machine-gunned on the beach at Gallipoli

22 Apr 1915 The Germans start using chlorine gas on their enemies

7 May 1915 British passenger ship the *Lusitania* is attacked by a German submarine and sinks. Over 1,000 passengers die, including some Americans – and America considers joining the war

31 May 1915 A German airship flies over London to drop bombs

1916 The world's first school for guide dogs for the blind opens in Germany

1 Jul 1916 The Battle of the Somme begins, after British shells fail to scare the Germans off. 60,000 British soldiers are killed or injured on a single day

Sep 1916 The British start using tanks in battle (but they're not very good yet)

Winter 1916	Germany's 'turnip winter' – so called because there was nothing else to eat
1917	The first blood bank is set up to help save wounded soldiers
Jan 1917	A huge blast destroys an explosives factory in London – along with 900 of its neighbours' houses!
Feb 1917	The Russians have a revolution and kick out their Tsar
6 Apr 1917	America joins in the war, on the side of the Allies
Nov 1917	Russia has another revolution and leaves the war
Apr 1918	The German air ace Baron von Richthofen is shot down and killed, having brought down eighty British planes during the war
Jun 1918	The Spanish Flu epidemic hits Europe and kills even more people than the war
8 Aug 1918	Hundreds of new, improved tanks make their appearance at the Battle of Amiens
Sep 1918	The Allies break through the Hindenburg Line and the Germans have to give in
Oct 1918	Carrier pigeon Cher Ami saves the lives of nearly 200 American soldiers on her last mission
11 Nov 1918	Germany and the Allies sign the armistice – an agreement that the war is officially over

QUIZ

1 Who killed Archduke Franz Ferdinand?
- the Black Hand Gang
- the Blue Nose Gang
- the Green Finger Gang

2 How many grandchildren
did Queen Victoria have?

YOUR COUNTRY NEEDS
"YOU"

3 Who was the man on the
'Your Country Needs You' poster?

4 What did all members of the British Army
have to grow in 1914?
- prize marrows
- Mohican hairdos
- moustaches

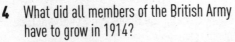

5 What do you call a spade if it's not a spade?

6 How did the French get emergency soldiers to the Front in 1914?

7 What shape were trenches built in?

8 What was the British royal family's surname before it was Windsor?

9 What were the women who worked in explosives factories called?

10 Which deadly weapon was invented by Hiram Maxim in the 1880s?

11 Why would soldiers wee on their own socks?

12 What were the big balloons called that were used before aeroplanes?

13 Why weren't pilots allowed to carry parachutes?
- because they were too heavy
- so they wouldn't jump out and waste a precious plane
- in case they didn't work

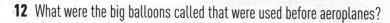

14 What was the colourful nickname of Baron Manfred von Richthofen?

15 What were German submarines called?

16 Who was 'the sick man of Europe'?

17 Where did T. E. Lawrence give money and guns to the locals?

18 Which terrifying animals were a danger to soldiers on the Eastern Front?

19 Which vehicle gave British boffins the idea for an armoured tank?

20 Which line did the Allies have to cross to win the war?

ANSWERS 1) The Black Hand Gang. 2) Forty. 3) Field Marshal Kitchener. 4) Moustaches. 5) An entrenching tool. 6) In taxicabs. 7) Zigzags. 8) Saxe-Coburg. 9) Canaries. 10) The machine gun. 11) To protect them from poison gas. 12) Airships. 13) So they wouldn't jump out and waste a precious plane. 14) The Red Baron. 15) U-boats. 16) The Ottoman Empire. 17) Arabia. 18) Wolves. 19) Tractors. 20) The Hindenburg Line.

155

Sir Tony Robinson's Weird World of Wonders is a multi-platform extravaganza (which doesn't mean it's a circus in a large railway station). You can get my World of Wonders game on line, there's a website, ebook, audio versions, extra stories and bits of weirdly wonderful design, marketing and publicity. In order to get all those things sorted out, I've surrounded myself with a grown-up version of the Curiosity Crew. They are Gaby Morgan and Fliss Stevens (Editorial), Dan Newman and Tracey Ridgewell (Design), Amy Lines (Marketing), Sally Oliphant (Publicity), James Luscombe (Digital), Tom Skipp (Ebooks) and Becky Lloyd (Audio).

A big thanks to them all; they are committed, funny and extremely cool.

Tony has to say that otherwise they'd stop work and go home!

Also available in this series